Summary
of

The Life We Bury
Allen Eskens

Conversation Starters

By BookHabits

Tips for Using BookHabits Conversation Starters:

EVERY GOOD BOOK CONTAINS A WORLD FAR DEEPER THAN the surface of its pages. The characters and their world come alive through the words on the pages, yet the characters and its world still live on. Questions herein are designed to bring us beneath the surface of the page and invite us into the world that lives on. These questions can be used to:

- Foster a deeper understanding of the book
- Promote an atmosphere of discussion for groups
- Assist in the study of the book, either individually or corporately
- Explore unseen realms of the book as never seen before

About Us:

THROUGH YEARS OF EXPERIENCE AND FIELD EXPERTISE, from newspaper featured book clubs to local library chapters, *BookHabits* can bring your book discussion to life. Host your book party as we discuss some of today's most widely read books.

Table of Contents

Introducing *The Life We Bury*

JOE TALBERT IS SLOGGING THROUGH LIFE, TRYING TO complete his assignments and earn enough money to put himself through college. He also has to deal with a bipolar and selfish mother who refuses to go to the doctor, and an autistic brother, Jeremy, for whom he feels responsible. What Joe does not need is a convicted murderer in his life, but this is exactly what happens when he signs up for a biography class. Unable to find anyone suitable, he accepts the suggestion of the nurse at the old age home to interview Carl Iverson, who had been convicted of the murder of a young girl thirty years ago. Now he has been released because of ill health, and the only person willing to talk to Joe for his assignment.

Once Joe talks to Carl, he gets involved in the story. Though reluctant at first, he realizes that this is a good way to spend time with Lisa, his neighbor, so he involves her in the project. Together, they unearth bits and pieces of Carl's history and realize that he was not the only suspect in the murder of Crystal Mary Hagen. Lisa and Joe gather together all the documents of the case and zero in on three suspects: Andy Fisher, Crystal's boyfriend at the time; Douglas Lockwood, Crystal's stepfather; and Danny Lockwood, Crystal's stepbrother.

Crystal Mary Hagen was a teenager who kept a diary, and most of the information unearthed about her came from this document. She lived in fear of her ultra-religious stepfather. She was an outgoing, cheerful girl but had to follow strict and unreasonable rules set by her stepfather, who held the threat of taking her out of her cheerleading team if she stepped out of line. She and her boyfriend were caught one day by her neighbor, Carl Iverson. This freaked Crystal out, and she was terrified of him telling her stepfather. She was also scared of Carl, whom she caught looking at her often and referred to him as a pervert in her diary. On the day of her murder, Crystal's mother was working, while Douglas and Danny were working in their garage. But what really stumps them is the code that Crystal used in some of her entries.

As the two dig deeper into the case, they begin to find proof of Carl's innocence. But this also means that the real murderer is walking scot-free. Though the authorities have agreed to help by reopening the case, Joe feels the need to solve the case and exonerate Carl before he dies, which leaves him very little time. As they close in on the real murderer, their lives are in danger because he is desperate enough to strike again. Ultimately, Lisa and Joe catch the murderer, exonerate Carl, and win an award of thousands of dollars, which they agree to share three ways between Joe, Lisa, and Jeremy. This enabled Joe to look after Jeremy, whom he had decided to rescue from their mother's neglect. After many years of putting up with his mother, he no longer has to, in a happy ending.

Discussion Questions

"Get Ready to Enter a New World"

Tip: Begin with questions dealing with broader issues to ensure ample time for quality discussions. Read through all discussion questions before engaging.

~~~

question 1

Once it becomes clear that Carl is probably innocent, whom did you suspect was the real murderer, and why?

~~~

~~~

question 2

Joe's mother was abusive and neglectful. How do you think that such a thing can be prevented, especially when it comes to autistic children? What other options do you think there was for Jeremy's care?

~~~

~~~

question 3

Joe and Lisa go on the chase together to catch a murderer who had run free for thirty years. Which one of them do you think was smarter and contributed more to the case, and why?

~~~

~~~

question 4

Carl Iverson did not protest his innocence vehemently during his trial or any time after. Why do you think he behaved like this? Do you think he wanted to die?

~~~

~~~

question 5

Virgil was Carl's friend in Vietnam, and he owed Carl his life. This is the reason Virgil strongly believed in Carl's innocence. Do you agree with this?

~~~

~~~

question 6

Carl sees a difference between murder and killing. What do you think the difference is? Do you agree that killing in a war is justified? Why or why not?

~~~

question 7

Joe was suffering from the guilt of not having been able to save his grandfather from drowning. Why do you think he felt redeemed by proving Carl innocent? What was the link he made between the two cases, according to you?

~~~

question 8

Virgil and Carl told Joe about their experiences with war and how it changed their lives. Do you think compulsory draft was necessary or a good thing? Why or why not?

~~~

~~~

question 9

What does the title "The Life We Bury" indicate? In what way is it connected to the plot of the book?

~~~

~~~

question 10

Joe and Lisa are amateurs who put their lives at risk to help Carl and find the truth about Crystal's murder. They were smart enough to find the culprit, but they also put themselves in danger. Do you think that they took some unnecessary risks? Which decision of theirs do you think was the worst thought out?

~~~

question 11

Douglas Lockwood was a religious fanatic who made Crystal's life miserable. He also helped his son Danny escape justice for rape and murder. Do you think he might have acted differently if he had not been a religious fanatic? How do you think he justified his actions with respect to his religious views?

~~~

question 12

How do you think Carl Iverson was treated in the nursing home where he lived? Was there any change in the way he was treated once his innocence was proved? How do you think people's attitude changed towards Carl after he was proved innocent?

~~~

question 13

The nurse told Joe that whenever she feels pity for Carl, she thinks of Crystal, the girl he was accused of brutally murdering. How do you feel about this? Do people deserve pity whether they committed terrible deeds or not? Is it possible to feel sorry for both the criminal and the victim? Can both their rights be protected? Discuss.

~~~

~~~

question 14

What purpose did the story of the Vietnamese girl serve? How well do you
think her story connects to the rest of the novel?

~~~

~~~

question 15

Why do you think Carl came across as a pervert to Crystal? Do you think decent men can have the appearance of being a pervert? How can men regulate their behavior to avoid this tag, and do you think they should have to?

~~~

~~~

question 16

Kirkus Reviews featured a review in which it calls *The Life We Bury* a thoughtful story. What do you find thoughtful about the book? What did you like most about the book?

~~~

~~~

question 17

The review in the blog *Mystery People* compares *The Life We Bury* to a Grisham thriller. Do you agree with this comparison? Why or why not? What similarities can you find between the books of Eskens and Grisham?

~~~

~~~

question 18

In a review, *Mystery People* says that the p*acing of The Life We Bury* is excellent. What do you think is meant by this? How does the pacing of the book propel the story forward in this case?

~~~

~~~

question 19

Mystery People published a review of *The Life We Bury* in which it claims that the reader begins to really care about the different characters. Did you feel this way? Which character did you identify with the most, and why?

~~~

~~~

question 20

In *Crime Fiction Lover*, the reviewer expresses their opinion that there is no way to tell that *The Life We Bury* is Allen Eskens' first book. Do you agree? Why or why not? What mistakes do authors generally make in their first books?

~~~

Introducing the Author

ALLEN ESKENS IS AN AMERICAN AUTHOR WHOSE FIRST book, *The Life We Bury*, was a hit. Compared to the stalwarts of the thriller genre such as John Grisham, Allen Eskens has firmly established himself with his debut book. He won the Rosebud Award for the Best First Mystery for his debut novel and was also a finalist for five more awards.

A lawyer by profession, Eskens was able to put in an extra dimension of his knowledge into his book. He had received his degree in journalism from the University of Minnesota and then graduated from Hamline University after completing his legal degree. He set up a practice in Minnesota and had been practicing law for more than twenty years before the writing bug bit him.

Eskens talks about his time in first grade when his teachers complained that he daydreamed too much. This was a common theme throughout his school years, but it was only when he was in college that he realized that he was actually telling stories in his mind. When he had to write a story for an assignment, he immediately took one of his daydreams and put it on paper, which impressed his teacher.

Eskens had been writing legal articles ever since he left law school, but he needed more knowledge and experience to write fiction. So he read books on fiction and attended creative writing classes and workshops at the Loft Literary Center and the Iowa Summer Writing Festival. Finally, he got his Masters in Fine Arts from Minnesota State University. After studying creative writing for a long time, he felt prepared to start writing his own book.

Currently, Eskens is still writing part time and has released his second novel. However, he feels he has now transitioned from a lawyer writing novels to a writer practicing law.

Fireside Questions

"What would you do?"

Tip: These questions can be a fun exercise as it spurs creativity among the readers by allowing alternate scene endings and "if this was you" questions.

~~~

question 21

The reviewer from the blog *Reactions to Reading* claims that the dark theme of the plot being offset by humorous and light moments made it more emotionally powerful. Do you agree? How do you think *The Life We Bury* could be made more emotionally powerful?

~~~

~~~

question 22

Reactions to Reading blog featured a review in which the reviewer claims that all the characters in the book are well drawn. Do you agree? Which character is your favorite, and why?

~~~

~~~

question 23

The review in the *Reactions to Reading* blog says that the book has a satisfactory conclusion. How do you feel about the conclusion? What do you think would have been a perfect ending?

~~~

~~~

question 24

In the *Book Journey* blog, the reviewer expresses their opinion that some bits of the story were predictable. Do you agree with this statement? Which parts do you think were predictable, and why?

~~~

~~~

question 25

In the *Book by Book* blog, the reviewer claims that *The Life We Bury* is an unusual kind of novel. What do you think they mean by this? Did you find the book unusual? Why or why not?

~~~

~~~

question 26

Eskens was an excellent legal writer, but he claims that writing fiction is very different. What is the difference, according to you?

~~~

~~~

question 27

Eskens claims that he has transitioned from a lawyer writing novels to a writer practicing law. What do you think he means by this statement? How does the way you identify yourself influence the work that you do?

~~~

~~~

question 28

Eskens says that his daydreaming as a child helped him develop as a writer. How do you think daydreaming can help someone? What other things do you think are required to be a good writer?

~~~

~~~

question 29

Eskens won an award for his first book and was the finalist for several other awards. What kind of pressure do you think this puts on an author when their first book is critically acclaimed and wins several awards?

~~~

~~~

question 30

Eskens has a three book deal and will be revisiting some of his old characters again. However, he has made it clear that he does not take well to the idea of an amateur sleuth stumbling over bodies again and again. What are the advantages and disadvantages of such a series?

~~~

~~~

question 31

Carl was ordered by his superior to rape a young Vietnamese girl, and he refused. How do you think you would have reacted to such an order during wartime? If you chose to follow the order, how would you have dealt with the guilt? If you chose not to follow the order, how do you think you would have handled the fallout?

~~~

question 32

Carl was innocent but did not care about being in prison, and he did not contribute much to his defense. If you were in his place, how much would you have wanted to help your defense team prove your innocence?

question 33

Douglas Lockwood chose to help his son escape justice for Crystal's death. If you were in his place, how would you have dealt with the situation, and why?

question 34

Crystal was scared of her stepfather because he was a religious fanatic and tried to keep her in line by restricting her basic freedoms, creating a toxic environment at home. Nothing much is mentioned about Crystal's mother, but if you were in her place, how much freedom would you have allowed your husband in disciplining your child? Discuss.

~~~

question 35

Joe's mother was unreliable and a slave to alcohol, though his autistic brother needed constant care. Joe finally decided to take charge of Jeremy in spite of all the difficulties he would have to face to look after an autistic brother. If you were Joe, what decision would you have made, and why?

~~~

~~~

question 36

Put yourself in Danny's place, in a position where you have committed the crime described in the book. How do you think you would react to it after the fact? Discuss.

~~~

question 37

Joe and Lisa don't think through the dangers and deliberately walk into danger in their quest to find the real killer of Crystal, instead of waiting for the authorities to get the evidence in the usual way. If you were them, which risks would you have chosen to take, and when would you have chosen to be cautious, and why?

~~~

question 38

Joe chose to interview a convicted murderer and rapist for his class assignment. If you were Joe, what kind of person would you find interesting to write about, and why?

~~~

Quiz Questions

"Ready to Announce the Winners?"

Tip: Create a leaderboard and track scores to see who gets the most correct answers. Winners required. Prizes optional.

~~~

quiz question 1

_____ killed Crystal.

~~~

~~~

quiz question 2

_____ protected Crystal's killer.

~~~

~~~

quiz question 3

_____ was the key to the code devised by Crystal.

~~~

~~~

quiz question 4

True or false: Carl raped the Vietnamese girl.

~~~

~~~

quiz question 5

The only person who believed in Carl's innocence was _____.

~~~

~~~

quiz question 6

True or false: Joe's mother was an alcoholic.

~~~

~~~

quiz question 7

_____ helped Joe hunt down the real killer.

~~~

quiz question 8

Eskens is a _____ by profession.

quiz question 9

Eskens got his bachelor's degree in _____.

quiz question 10

Eskens won the _____ for the Best First Mystery.

~~~

quiz question 11

The Life We Bury is Eskens'_____ book.

~~~

~~~

quiz question 12

Eskens studied creative writing for more than _____ years before he was
ready to write a novel.

~~~

Quiz Answers

1. Danny Lockwood
2. Douglas Lockwood
3. "The quick brown fox jumps over the lazy dog." This sentence contains all the letters of the alphabet and is hence used for typing practice, a skill that Crystal had recently picked up.
4. False; he disobeyed the orders of his superior to rape the girl.
5. Virgil
6. True
7. Lisa
8. Lawyer
9. Journalism
10. Rosebud Award
11. First
12. Twenty

Ways to Continue Your Reading

EVERY month, our team runs through a wide selection of books to pick the best titles for readers and reading groups, and promotes these titles to our thousands of readers – sometimes with free downloads, sale dates, and additional brochures.

Want to register yourself or a book group? It's free and takes 1-click.

Register here.

On the Next Page...

Please write us your reviews! Any length would be fine but we'd appreciate hearing you more! We'd be SO grateful.

Till next time,

BookHabits

"Loving Books is Actually a Habit"

Made in the USA
San Bernardino, CA
16 August 2018